KEEP GOD in MIND

LARRY GENE BAXTER SR.

ISBN 979-8-88943-925-7 (paperback)
ISBN 979-8-88943-926-4 (digital)

Christian Faith Publishing
832 Park Avenue
Meadville, PA 16335
www.christianfaithpublishing.com

Printed in the United States of America

My name is Larry Gene Baxter, and everybody calls me *Possum*. I was called by God when I was eight or nine years old. He called me by my nickname *Possum*, and it scared me. I ran up the steps and fell, and it put a mark on my leg. I said, "Mama, something called my name." I didn't know that it was God until I grew up. I went through all kinds of sickness and danger, and I did all kinds of sins, but I never hated another human being. I'd always loved everybody.

I stopped schooling at sixth grade. And I was just as smart as a person that went to college because I was taught by God. He taught me common sense. But I will tell everyone to get a good education because life ain't very sweet without it. But read some of The Thi__ that God taught me. I can tell you all about the Bible and how it tricks the world. I will give you all something to think about so you all can keep on reading. If God drowned the world, then he would be a sinner himself. Keep reading, and you will see some of the things that God taught me. God is good all the time.

The devil tricked the whole world with the Bible, telling us that God killed and said that he was the Savior so we could call on him and he could get our soul. The devil blinds the world with the Bible. How else? He is going to get souls. The devil lies to the world. But that is the devil's job—telling lies to make people think he's telling the truth. But he has to use another name. People always say God is good all the time, but they believe that lie about God drowning the world. That will be wrong, and God can't do no wrong because he is good all the time.

In the Bible, it says that God created Adam and Eve. And it says that they didn't know that they were naked until they ate some fruit. Then their eyes opened. If you were blind, would you know whether you were naked or not? And they were partners. They had to do number one or two, so they should know that they didn't have clothes to pull up or down. It is also said in the Bible that Cain killed Abel and God told Cain to go to another city and he would put a mark on his head so people would know him. If Adam and Eve were the only people here, where did all the other people come from? When God told Cain to go to that city, the devil was just writing a book.

The devil knows that when a person dies, they turn to dust. That was why he said God made man out of dust. Hey, the devil brainwashed a lot of people with the Bible. The devil is the master of telling lies. He will fool you with that Bible. He'll have you believing all kind of lies. The biggest lie he told in the Bible was when he said that he was God's son and God was a killer. Lying on God, it ain't nobody better than God. We could've picked a better creator than God. God is a true and loving God all the time. I bet you if God comes right now and tell people, "You never knew me," a lot of people will be in trouble. You gotta get to know God because he's good all the time. He is the best thing that ever happened to us—the one and only one.

People, use common sense and think about what you read. The Bible says that God drowned the world. That means that he drowned little babies and kids and everybody. God knew that we were going to sin before he put us here. God wouldn't kill his kids; God loved us. Then it says that God closed the sea on Moses' enemy. It also says that God turned around and wrote the Ten Commandments, including "thy shall not kill," when it just said that he drowned the world and killed Moses' enemy.

Think about when it said God drowned the world and saved the animals. We are talking about a couple thousands of animals. They say that an elephant eats three hundred pounds of food and drinks fifty gallons of water a day. And lion and other big cats eat all kind of different raw meat of other animals. Where did they get all that food from to feed a couple thousands of animals for forty days and forty nights? The devil lied on God. Think about it. If God did something like that, then he would be a sinner himself. And we know that God can't sin. Wake up, people. The devil is tricking people with that book, which he calls the Bible, and telling people that he's the Savior so people can come to him and he can get their soul.

Jesus said that he would be with us to the ends of the world. Why did Jesus say that he'd be with us to the ends of the world? It was because he was going to burn. And he wanted us to burn with him. You see, with God, there is no end. See how the devil know so much? He fooled us with the Bible and told us he was God's son, Jesus, so we could tell him what we knew because he didn't know anything until we would tell him.

In the Bible, it says that Jesus raised people from the dead. But the Bible never said that he raised a person from the grave. The devil thought we would never figure that out. Think about what he said: he was raised from the dead but not from the grave. So, people, put it together. He just messes with your mind. He just wants people to call on him, and he wants people to think that he is God's son. Don't fall for that; he is the devil. He now fools a lot of people with that Bible. So, people, wake up. If you don't, he is going to steal your soul.

If you all think about it, he said he did better than God. Everybody ought to know that is a lie. I'm not better than no one else. You can have all the money in the world, but you ain't better than a person that lives in a paperboard box because we are all a child of God. You all might read and write better than me, but when it comes to common sense, it's hard to beat me because I have learned from the best—God. I pray and talk to God a lot. So many people call on Jesus, but one day, they are going to find out that they have been wrong. You see, the devil has to come up with some, so he put it in a book. He got people thinking it is a true book.

The devil wrote the Bible, telling us that God had relation with someone else's woman in a spiritual way. He lied that God impregnated someone else's woman. God won't mess with someone else's woman. God can create a woman for himself. The devil could not tell us that he was God's brother or sister because God didn't have a mother or father. That was why the devil lied that he was God's son Jesus. The devil had to come up with a lie to get our soul. That was why he said to come to him. He didn't want us to go to God.

The devil is a smart liar. He tells lies to make us think that he is telling the truth. In the Bible, words about Jesus are easy to read and sound good, and when you read about God, it sounds dangerous and scary. All those are lies about God. God is a good God. God is good all the time, and God can do everything except to fail. Everything in the Bible talks bad about God and talks good about Jesus. The devil had to write a book to make himself look good. That was why he used another name and told people that he was God's son so we could call on him too. He tried to make God look bad. He told us that God drowned the world and did all that killing so we wouldn't go around talking and preaching about God. The devil wanted us to go around preaching and talking about him. That was why he wrote the Bible telling us that he is God's son Jesus. Jesus is the devil. He has people calling on him before they call on God. He got people praising him. He gets people to read the Bible about God giving man strength to push a building down on people.

The devil wrote that Bible, telling all the lies about God. You see, he lied that God is his father, and when we read about Jesus in the Bible, little kids can read it. A college person can't read about God all them name about fifty pages nothing but names. You get to turn pages, then it says God killed somebody—that's lying on God. God won't kill a fly. If Jesus was God's son, why didn't he stay here with us? He couldn't die no more. The devil made things seem true in the Bible so he could get our soul. You see, the devil can't do no more than we let him. That was why he said he was God's son.

The devil said that God is a killer, and he is the Savior. Think about it. Do you all think that God had a relationship with someone else's woman? In a spiritual way, God can create a woman for himself. The first woman could have been God. He's always been here. The devil Jesus knew that he couldn't prove that he was God's son. That was why he said that he left in the clouds. He's still in the clouds. He is the devil, trying to make people think he has left in the cloud and went to heaven. That one day, he's going to come in the clouds and people are going to run to him and call him Jesus, and all hell is going to break loose.

The devil Jesus is in the clouds, and he can make rain, he can make the lighting, and he can make tornado and earthquake. He can make people go to war. He also can make a baby and have babies. But he can't tell us when the world is going to end. That is another reason why he said God was his father because he knows that God created the world and God knew when to stop it. The devil is blue in the clouds. But in the Bible, it is mentioned that Moses said, "God, let me see you."

And God said, "I'll show you my body. It was blue."

The devil Jesus is blue in the cloud. The devil switches it around. God has eyes like ball of fire, feet like brass, and hair like sheep wool. The devil had to write a book to get people to call on him. None of the people have a last name. Jesus said a donkey had a cross on its back because he rode a donkey. A donkey had a cross on its back when God created them. The devil was just saying that to make people think that he was God's son so people could call on him. That was because he wanted souls.

In the Bible, it says if your eyes caused you to sin, you should pluck them out. God will be the only one with eyes because he can't sin. The devil gets people thinking that God is a killer, and he is the savior. It ain't but two good and a bad. God is good, and the devil is bad. The devil can't get no soul by telling people that he is bad. He had to use another name. That was why he told people that his name was Jesus. Jesus said that we were going to be judged in the cloud. If he died for our sins, why should we be judged? If he is God's son. Jesus said that those without sin must cast the first stone.

He caused sin on everyone. He wrote that Jesus also said the gate to hell was wide and lot of people would find it. He said that because a lot of people believed that he was God's son. That's not God's son; that's the devil. He said that the gate to heaven was narrow a few would find it. He said that because very few knew that he ain't God son. Think about it. The devil ain't said nothing bad about himself. That was why he used another name to make himself look good. He used the name Jesus. The devil didn't want us calling on God.

I'm going to ask you all something. If you all have the power to make it rain, would you all drown the world—little babies, kids, and everybody but save the animals? No, you won't, and God didn't either. That book will fool you, and that was how lies got out about God. Don't believe the Bible and what it says about God. God won't hurt or kill us; we are his kids. God loves us, and he doesn't want us to kill each other. What makes people think God will kill us? God is perfect. God doesn't have no evil in him. God is a sweet God, and God is with us even if we are good or bad. We are still his kids. We are going to make mistakes because we are not God. God is a forgiving God. He knows what we are going to do before he puts us here. The devil tells people how the world was created. The devil doesn't know how the world was created.

God created the world in front of the devil's face, and the devil still doesn't know how God did it. God is the Creator, and God can create the world in one second. The world has never been destroyed. God won't destroy anything he created. The devil talked about himself when he said that Jesus beat the devil. He wanted us to say that Jesus had beaten the devil so we could call on him. He was talking about himself. The Bible says about the devil Jesus saying he can do the same as God. Then he said, "I will trick them and tell them I'm God's son so they can come to me." The devil tries to make the Bible sound true so we can believe that he is God's son.

Hey, no one gets to believe me, so don't get mad at me. But I was called by God. Love and faith are the way to God. The devil wants us to have faith in God the size of a mustard seed; that ain't no faith at all. That is like telling God, "I got a little faith in you the size of a mustard seed." All God done for us and still doing for us. Have faith in God. I talk to people all the time about God, and some call me crazy. But they believe the Bible telling them that God drowned the world and did all that killing. The devil knows that none of us was here, so he wrote the Bible telling lies like God is a killer and that he is the Savior. A lot of people fell for it. If God was a killer, then he wouldn't be a good God. I say that God is good all the time. God doesn't have no wrong in him.

You see, the devil can do all kinds of things, like making flood and all snowstorms, and then he puts it in your mind that God is doing it; he lies, just like about God drowning the world. But God is good. Don't believe that lie like God drowned the world and messed with someone else's woman. None of us was here. But people believe a book telling them that God killed. Hey, the devil can write a book. He can make it sound so true. That is why I tell everyone to keep God in mind because the devil will put all kinds of things in your mind. He will try to keep us from thinking about God. But if you all think about it, in the Bible, it says that God picked animals over people. It says that God drowned people and saved the animals. It all so says there will be fire the next time. What is God going to do—save the fishes and snake? Telling lies on God.

You all need to know that the devil wrote the Bible. So, people, get your life together because the devil is trying to steal your soul. Take a good look at how he gets a lot of people do all kinds of sin. He gets a lot of people praying to him. So keep on reading, and you will see what I'm talking about. You see, there are two sides to every story. And the Bible have two sides too. Hey, you all should know that God doesn't do no wrong. Hey, the devil can kill people, but he's not going to tell us that he can kill. Instead, he tells a lie that God will kill. The devil ain't going to say nothing good about God. That why you need to have all faith in God because the Bible ain't say nothing good about God.

I didn't write this book to make money off it. I just wanted people to get right with God because Jesus got just about everybody calling on him. The devil Jesus now made hell on earth. He got a lot of words in the Bible sound so true. But that is his job—to fool people so he can get their soul. If he had everything sounding like a lie, you all would figure him out. He is the master of telling lies. He had you all believe all kinds of lies, and some of the things he said sounded good. But that is his game plan so he can get all your souls. But think about it. In the Bible, it says God saved Noah and his family. What God say, hell with the baby and kids and everyone else. Lying on God. God ain't no evil God. God is love. But like I said, I told people that God called me. But people called me crazy; they said that was a demon calling me. But they believed that God talked to Noah and Moses. All of the names are make-believe in the Bible. None of us was here, but they believed that lying book about God killing all the people. I don't care how much wrong we do; God still won't hurt us because he can't do no wrong and because he is good all the time. Hey, God loves us, and he is our father. I don't care if people never know. For me, I want people to know God because he is the Creator. He will never turn his back on us. He's not a back turner. God is good, you all. I ain't telling no lie; he's good.

God is a true God, and he is a loving God. I'm going to tell you all why the devil made so many different races of people—to hate Black people more. That is because God is a Black man. Don't believe in me; believe in God. But believe in the word I'm saying if you want to be saved. Believe in this book because God told me to write this book. It doesn't take a lot of words to tell the truth.

Jesus said in the Bible all these bad things are going to happen before the world comes to an end. If he was God's son, why would he let these bad things to happen to us before he would come? Then he said it ain't going to end right now. Jesus is the devil. He wants bad things to happen to us. He is fulfilling what he wrote. People calling on Jesus gives him power to do it. But one day, God is going to stop it. People sing and pray to Jesus. But the Bible tells us that God is a killer. Think about it. The devil tricks the world with a book telling lies on God and trying to make himself look good, but he has to use another name. The devil Jesus makes things seem true in the Bible so we can believe he is God's son. Jesus told us that he healed the sick and raised the dead. He didn't say that God healed the sick because he didn't want God to have our souls. He tells us that God drowned the world and he's going to set it on fire—lying on God. God is good all the time. God will never turn his back on us. I'm going to ask you all man something. If you have the power to create people, will you impregnate somebody else's woman when you can create a woman for yourself?

The devil tells lies like hurricane have a sudden time to come. He brings hurricane about the same time all the time to keep us from thinking he is doing it. Just like he said to have faith in God the size of a mustard see—that ain't no faith at all. If God asks you if you have faith in him, what are you going to say? A little faith the size of a mustard seed? God is good. But think about this. The devil Jesus got to say in the Bible that he was walking on the water to reach his hand out to the man. And when the man stared to sink, Jesus said, "what little faith." He wanted people to have a lot of faith in him but have little faith in God, the size of a mustard seed. You see, that is a make-believe book. It sounds so true. That is the devil's game plan so he can get your soul. He got just about everybody on earth calling on him—the devil Jesus.

He puts himself before God, but you all need to know that nobody comes before God. Good as God is do you all believe that God drowned little baby's and kids. There is no love greater than God's love. You see, the devil Jesus will kill, but he didn't put it in the Bible. But he gets that lie in the Bible that God kills because he wants us to think that about God. It says in the Bible the good gets to suffer with the bad. Why? That is because the good and the bad think Jesus is God's son, and people are praying to him. But believe this: if you all think God drowned the world and did all that killing, you all are going to miss out on God one day—that is no lie. Jesus is the devil. He gets to make it sound true so you can believe it, and he can get your soul. The devil Jesus knows what to say so people will call and pray to him. He ain't going to say nothing good about God. He would tell you all that God drowned the world and did all that killing because ain't no one is going to preach about that.

The devil Jesus got in the Bible that he healed the sick, made the blind see, and raised the dead. He got people believing that, and he got in the Bible about God drowning the world. Like I said, we were talking about little babies, kids—everybody, and God picked animal over little babies and kids, and God drowned them. God is good all the time. It also says God told Noah that he was going to drown the world. He was going to save the animal and drown the little babies and everyone, and some people believe that lie. Where did they get lumber and electric from billion and billions of years ago? With thousands of animals, no one could stay in there because of the smell—telling lies on God. It says in the Bible that everybody did better than God. You all should know that ain't no one better than God; the Bible is a make-believe book. Think about it. Little kids knocking at the door of the ark, and Noah would say, "God has the key, and you can't get in." But the Bible says he saved the animals. These are all lies on God.

I talk to God all the time, and sometimes, I don't sleep. People, God is smart, and he know everything because he is the Creator. Everything God created is smart, so you know God is smart. God didn't drown the world. God didn't have a relationship with someone else's woman in a spiritual way. Jesus is not God's son—that is the devil. He got it in the Bible that Jesus ain't did no wrong, got it in the bible that God did all kind of wrong. If you think about it, lying on God. The devil got some things that sounds true in the Bible so you all can think he's God's son, and so you all can call on him and pray to him.

In the Bible, it says that a man saw Jesus walking on the water. He thought it was a ghost, but it was Jesus. Jesus reached out his hand out to the man, then the man started to sink, and Jesus said, "What little faith." But in the Bible, Jesus wanted us to have faith in God the size of a mustard seed. That ain't no faith at all; you just can't see a mustard seed. Jesus wanted us to have a lot of faith in him. People, you all need to watch that devil; he's trying to trick you. He wants us to think that he can do the same as God. But he had to use another name; he used the name Jesus. He's trying to make our life a living hell on earth. A lot of people might have a lot of money, but he doesn't care. As long as you think he is God's son Jesus, he still got you. Rich or poor if you calling on Jesus.

In the Bible, Jesus told the little kids to come to him because he wanted their souls too. He said that he fed so many people with a couple fish and a loaf or a bread. God created the fish and thought the Bible could offer God a goat and a bull. If you all think about it, the devil was Jesus trying to make God look bad in the Bible. God has always been here, and that is why the Bible says that God had a relationship with someone else's woman two thousand and some years ago. If God had made a man like that, he would tell us to go to God first because God is the Creator. Bottom line, people are calling on Jesus before they call on God.

Everything you all ask Jesus for, he's coming back with the rain and tornado to destroy it. He is trying to make hell on earth, so when he comes in the clouds so we can go down with him. So get your life together and turn to God. I got my life together, and I will only call on God. Some people believe in a book. Ain't God good all the time? Well, why do people believe the Bible saying that God drowned the world? None of us was here when the Bible was written. The devil tells us anything to get his name out there. The devil has to get people to call on him. Jesus said he's going to prepare a place for us. Where he'll be, that's where we'll be also. If he is God's son, why can't we go with him when he prepares a place for us? The Bible says it is easy for a camel to get through an eye of a needle than a rich person to get to heaven. If that is true, why is everyone trying to get rich?

Back on Jesus. Jesus said ain't no one going to know when he comes. That's because he is the devil. He wants us to be sinning when he comes. You all might read some of the same thing in this book over and over, and that's because I want you all to know that God doesn't do no wrong. But if you all think about it, the Bible says that God killed more people than the world wars one and two, and everyone should know that is a lie. It says Jesus said that he can do the same as God. But the Bible says he did better than God. And you all know that's a lie. No one is better than God. He lies that God drowned the world.

In the Bible, God killed all the first-born boys. Now, the devil is trying to set the earth on fire and trying to make people think that God is doing it. That's the devil's doing. We are God's kids, and God wants us to come to him. If God is a jealous God, why do people call on Jesus? The Bible is a make-believe book. When you all read the book of Revelation, it says God is going to have angels in four corners. That sounds like some the devil will have, just like the Bible talking about the seven seals. That sounds scary. God doesn't have anything that will scare us because God is good. God has nothing like that. It sounds like something the devil has. People, get your life together. God is good to us. It ain't no love greater than God's love.

The devil can come as people and talk to you about Jesus, who he is. They ain't going to say nothing good about God because they can be false prophets trying to get soul for Jesus. But if you all think God drowned the world and killed people, you all don't know God at all. All you have to say is, "God, I was wrong. Forgive me," and he will because he is a forgiving God. The Bible tells you that God helped Daniel and Jacob. Those names in the Bible are make-believe. The devil got people to believe in what he wrote. We were not here, and some people believe it. The devil had to come up with something to get us to call on him. He got the whole world thinking he's God's son Jesus. The devil had to come up with a lie so people can pray and call on him. How else could the devil get us to call on him? He had to use another name. The devil put himself in the clear.

You see, years ago, people only called on God until they learn how to read. Then they say God got a son. Those names in the Bible, the devil made them up. He had to make it sound good so you would believe in him. The devil tricked people with the Bible. You all get the Bible and sit down and think about it. Ask yourself, "Did God do this, killing all those people? And you will find out that's a lying book. So get your life together and serve God or the devil. The devil lied that God is a killer, and he is the Savior. That's what that lying book says. The devil tells lies all the time, and I've caught him.

The devil Jesus said the water obeyed him, but he used it to hurt us. But he left us a Bible so we could read about him. The devil can make you have all kinds of dreams. But he gets it in the Bible that a man knows what your dream is about. The devil knows because he makes you dream it. The devil knows everything because we tell him and because he told us that his name is Jesus.

Look at the world today. Since people been calling on Jesus, he's been making hell on earth. Because he is the devil, he gets in your heart and mind. When you call on him or even if you don't call on him, he'll still put things in your mind. If you all call on God and believe in God, you all will be saved. Don't believe that Bible and what it says God did. Like I've said, if Jesus was God's son, why didn't he stay here with us? What he said was he would be with God and leave us down here with the devil. Jesus is the devil. If I'm lying, I am hoping God lets everyone live except me. Let me burn forever. But I'm not lying because God is not a killer. God is a good all the time. God is with us, even if we are good or bad. He won't turn his back on us. Love covers all sins because God is love. If you want to preach and talk about God, you have to do it from the heart because that's where God looks at—our heart. Because the Bible didn't tell you nothing about God. I don't care how bad your sin is; God will forgive you for it because he is a forgiving God. Because he is the Creator, he knows what you are going to do even before you do it.

All you have to do is ask him to forgive you and don't do it anymore. God gave us the knowledge to be anything we want to be. We are God's children, and he will never turn his back on us; he will never hurt us. God loves us, and God is good. He knows everything we are going to do before he puts us here. God sees and hears everything. Some people get sick, and God heals them. Who do they think Jesus is? God has all the power. Jesus told people that He had all the power so the people could call on him. It is time to put a stop to that devil Jesus. I am the man who will put a stop to him because I was called by God, and that is the truth. I ain't lying my lying days are over. You will never get right with God. Call on Jesus because Jesus is the devil. That's who you are getting right with.

If Jesus is God's son, he isn't suppose put himself before God. Nobody comes before God. You see, Jesus is the devil. He wants us to call on him before we call on God. Jesus has had people praying to God in his name. That is why he said to come to him. Your biggest sin is calling on Jesus. Jesus told his disciples in the Bible to go and speak his word. He really was telling us to go speak his word so we could help him get souls. You know, some Bibles have red-written texts when you read about Jesus. He doesn't want you to miss nothing.

When I was reading the Bible, it didn't make no sense. When I used to call on Jesus, it used to mess with my mind. I used to say, "Some ain't right about this book." It said that Jesus did better than God, and I knew that was a lie. Ain't no one is better than God. God can do all that healing because he is the Creator. Do you all think that God will drown little babies that did no wrong? God is good. God won't kill nobody. If you all think that God could kill, then you all don't know God at all. So get to know him because he is a true God, not like that lying devil.

Think about all those people that the devil has tricked. He has fooled people that he's God' son Jesus. He has had people thinking that he's God's son so he can get their soul. If you all think about it, he had it in the Bible that God was an evil God. The devil hates us, but he hates God more. He made himself look good in the Bible and made God look like a killer. You see, I know so much about the devil because I used to run with him when I was in the street, thinking he was God's son. Now, I run with God. Now, I know a lot about God. God wants us to know about him because he doesn't have anything to hide. He is a good and true God all the time. He is a loving God.

Think about it. If you were God and I was the devil, you knew I would talk bad about you so people would come to me. But the people ain't going come to me if I used the name devil, so I had to use another name as long as I had people call me on the name Jesus.

The devil makes you think you are doing good, but if you start calling on just God, he will try to mess with you mind so people will think that you are crazy. But God is good, and you all know that the Bible ain't right when it says that God did more killing than anybody in the Bible. It says that God killed body and soul; that's lying on God. *God, if I'm wrong about anything, forgive me because only you know everything.*

The Bible said that God didn't know the world was going to do all that sin. Like I said, God knows everything, and God knows that we are going to sin before he created us. But the devil lied that people caused sins in the world. The devil caused people to sin because he is a lying devil, telling lies on God. God will never turn his back on us. He never has and he never will; we are God's kids. So, people, start praying to God and only God because he is a loving God and a true God.

I wrote this book because I got God in me and God is the only one that I pray to, and I was called by God. I feel good all the time, and I don't let nothing worry me because God is a problem solver, and I have my life together. People don't come to see me because the devil is not going to send them and because the devil doesn't want them to hear the truth. So get your life together because God sees and hears everything. God is good all the time, and that the truth and nothing but the truth. But the devil had some people believe all kinds of lies. He had people thinking the Bible is a true book. He had people thinking that God killed people. But Jesus had something sounding true in the Bible so people think he is God's son.

God didn't make no man that can do the same as he can. God is God alone, and I was called by God to speak his words, and God put it in my mind what he had to say. Like one time, a guy asked me what God couldn't do. I had never heard it before, and God brought it out of my mouth. I said "God can't fail." I have been speaking God's words for about ten years. I have never asked anyone for one cent because God's word is free. These people speaking about Jesus, they are getting your money and setting you up for the devil, who is Jesus. But Jesus tells us to love one another. He doesn't care as long as we call on him. Then Jesus says he doesn't know when the world is going to end. If he is God's son, then he should know when it going to end. He says he can do the same as God. But if you sit back and think about what you read, you will catch the devil in all kinds of lies.

I used to read the Bible about God. I used to say that God was mean, killing all those people. I used to say that I was scared to meet God. He might cut my head off for all the sins I did. Then I looked back at all the danger that I went through, and I wasn't get hurt. Then I said that Bible has been lying on God. All the sins that I did, he didn't kill me. The Bible says that God drowned little babies and kids and everybody. Little kids ain't did no wrong. And the Bible says that God drowned them. I knew that's a lie. But if the Bible was a true book, God wouldn't want us to read things that happened millions and millions of years ago.

Then if you think about it, the Bible tells us that God couldn't handle the people, so he drowned them and saved animals. Then here came Jesus saying God so loved the world that he gave his only begotten son. Now, this was where he fooled you, with believe in God also believe in him. He has been lying to us. God doesn't make mistakes because he is the Creator. I thank you, God, for never giving up on us. God, you are good to us all the time. Thank you. I ain't telling no lie. Thank you, God. You ain't never kill no one. You don't care how bad we are; you are still good to us. God, you know all about us. God, we are glad that you are our Creator. We are your kids, and you are better to us than we are to ourself and to people most of the time.

I talk to God all day and night. I talk to God more than I talk to my wife. So my brothers and my sisters, don't feel ashamed. I stopped schooling at sixth grade because God knew I was going to stop at sixth grade. God brought me and everyone else a mighty long way. Don't never give up on God because if we do our best, God will do rest. People, I am saved by God. He is the only one that can save you. When you think there is no way, God will make a way because he is a waymaker. But Jesus telling people that he is the way, he is the way to hell. Since I have found out that Jesus is the devil, he's been putting all kinds of sins in my mind like what I used to do. But it doesn't worry me because I know God has now forgiven me. But as long as you believe in Jesus, he will make you think that you are doing good. Soon as you find out he is the devil, he will have you hear voices and see things. He'll try to make people think that you are crazy. He had me doing all kinds of sins, but he couldn't ever make me hate another human being.

But when I used to believe in Jesus, I never did call on him. I always have put God first. It ain't nobody come before God—not me, not anyone. I love God, you all, and he has always saved me and healed me and forgave me. God is good to us all the time. Hey, people always call on Jesus but think about it. People wear crosses around their neck, and that is the devil sign. But you know, they burn crosses in people's yards. I say I know something ain't right. I know what I'm talking about. I talk to a lot of people, and they think I'm crazy. But one day, when that devil comes down from the clouds, it is going to be hell on earth. I tell people that God called me when I was a kid, and he might call me again, and then I will know what to do. I pray to get this book out there one day. People, it's time to make a change. The devil has been leading people the wrong way for a long time, telling people that the Bible is a true book. He's trying to get souls any way he can. In the Bible, the devil Jesus ain't say one time that he killed someone, but that's he was the one doing all that killing with fires and floods and earthquakes. God lets so much happen to show people that it ain't his doing because he doesn't kill.

Jesus is the devil, and he fools a lot of people. When he says that he died and came back, and he said look to at the hole in his hands. Hey, a liar can tell a lie and make it sound true. We are living in hell, and it is going to get worst when the devil Jesus comes down from the cloud. All hell is going to break lose because everybody calls on Jesus, thinking that he is God's son. The only way out is God. Hey, I might be the way out because I was called by God, and he might call me again. No one believes me, but I hope you all do because I'm not telling a lie, and that's the truth. We all are a child of God. But a lot of people now gives their life to Jesus, thinking that he is God's son. When I used to go to church, I used to believe Jesus was God's son. But I never did call on Jesus before I call on God. I always put God first. But now, I know that ain't God's son. Now I only call on God. My life started to change, and I see all the blessings that God has given me. Think about it. The devil Jesus can bless you if you call on him, and he knows one day it ain't going to do you no good because he is going to come back with flood and tornado and fire and destroy it. But when God gives you something, the devil can't destroy it. If you call on Jesus, he will make you think that you are sitting on top of the world. When I used to run around, I thought I was doing good. When God stopped me from running around, I thought I was going down.

But God picked me up—no lie. God stopped me because when you think there was no way, God would make a way out of it. Hey, I'm trying to see how far I can go with a sixth-grade education. But I learned a lot with common sense; it took me a long way. By me talking to God every day and night, riding or walking, I learned a lot. God helped me to figure out that Bible. Hey, just look in the Bible and read it. Think about it, and you will see that the Bible has another side, and this book I'm writing is the other side—that is no lie. I know there's no way God did what that Bible said he did because he is a loving and a true and a good God. And he can't fail, and you all know he can't fail.

If you think about it, all that the Bible says that God did was fail, and that's a lie. We all sin, and God knows that we are going to sin before he puts us here. What he is going to do set us on fire. Jesus wrote in the Bible telling all lies about God, and he said all good things about himself. And a lot of people fell for that lie. I'm telling you all to get yourself together before Jesus pops up in the clouds. I know what I'm talking about. Jesus said that he died for our sin. He said that he did all that for us so we could call on him before we could call on God. Jesus had people calling on him, and he is the devil. The devil Jesus got the whole world fighting. If Jesus was God's son, why wouldn't he stop it? He can't stop it; only God can stop it. That was why Jesus lied that God was his father. God is the only one who can stop it. God still gives people a chance to call on him. God won't let you down; you can always depend on him. One thing about God is that you can always talk to him.

Then some people said that they found Jesus's tomb. Jesus put that in some people's mind to tell that lie, just like when they said they found the ark. The devil was trying to make people think that God destroyed the world. God will never kill us. He doesn't have that in him because God is the *truth* and the *light*. God is our Savior. The devil Jesus lied that he's the *truth* and the *light* and the *savior*. Hey, I never did believe in the Bible. I thought I was doing wrong by not believing in the Bible, but I was doing right by not believing in the Bible. God ain't no dirty God. If I'm wrong, throw me in a lake or fire, and let me burn forever. But I will tell you it will never happen because I know God, and I know who the devil is. Think about it. When it rains for one day, it almost covers your house up. But the Bible says God made it rain for forty days and forty nights. And people believe God did something like that. If something like that happened, the devil would try that. But God wouldn't let the devil destroy his kids. Think about this: how could they stay on the ark with that smell for forty days and forty nights, with animals doing numbers one and two? If you had a chance to save a little baby or a lion from drowning, which one will you save? I will save the baby. The Bible says God drowned the little babies and everyone else and saved the animal—all lies about God.

I didn't write no big book with a lot of pages because it doesn't take a lot to get to know God and who the devil is. In the Bible, it says that Jesus ain't never did no wrong. He is a lying devil. But God is the only one that never did no wrong because he is good all the time. The Bible have two sides. The Ten Commandments say thy shall have no other God, but people are calling on Jesus like he is God. Get your life together because hell is on earth. I don't care if you are rich or poor. If you are calling on Jesus, you are going to catch hell one day because he is the devil. Jesus said that he is God's son. He said that he died for our sins. What that meant was we could keep on sinning. I'm going to end this book, but I'm going to leave this with you. You can make hell on earth. The choice is yours. But think about it, if God made a place up there in the sky called heaven, we would be up there with him. He wouldn't leave us down here with the devil. God is right here with us. The devil is finished and will come to an end, and God will put his name right here on earth. So who are you all going to serve, God or Jesus? So if I'm wrong, forgive me.

One time, a snake went up my pants. And I had one of my mother's dress over my head, acting like a ghost and getting at my brother and sisters. I ran into the house and busted a vein in my nose. I bled for hours, and there was no other house around, and we didn't have a car or phone. I had to sit there for hours and wait for my mother to get off from work. One time, I was walking barefoot and I stepped on a bee, and my feet swelled up like an elephant foot. Like I said, I stopped at sixth grade, and my mother and father didn't get no education. Our mother and father had fourteen kids together. My father had thirty kids in total. My mother was my father's second wife, and she was twenty years younger than our father.

I am the twenty-fifth kid out of thirty kids. I got a job when I was fifteen, and I got hurt on the job. I got some money out of a deal, and my mother told me to buy that old house we were staying in. I said, "Mama, you love money."

And she said, "Baby, I don't love money. I just want to keep a roof over your head and some food to eat."

I said something like that to our mother. She was good to us. Later on, our mother died, and before she died, she told me, "Possum, you can't love just me. You got to love everybody."

I bought that house before she died. I bought that house when I was fifteen. When our mother died, I was in the yard. That was the first time I called on God. I went through life having fun, loving everybody, and working those dangerous jobs. One day, on the way to work, a truck in front of us had cement block on the back. One of the blocks fell off and got under the truck, and the truck that we were in turned us over down a hill. We turned over about ten or fifteen times or more. One job I had, I was running a chipper. It ground up logs and turned them into chips. I ran that job for a couple of years, and I like to go in the chipper over a thousand times, and nobody would know what happened to me.

Then I did another job. It was dangerous that as I was running a machine picking up logs one or two o'clock in the morning, I would fall asleep in the machine. Chain he running kicking logs in my face about to knock my head off. I would wake up and throw it back, and that happened all through the days and nights. I thought I was that good running the jobs, but God was saving me all the time. I was just working and running around and didn't even thank God. I was working those dangerous jobs, and God was saving me every day and night, and I was having fun, giving people my money and taking my family and friends out to have a good time.

One time, we went to the lake to swim, and the water took me out in middle of the lake, and my feet were no longer touching the ground. I said, "I will go ahead and ground." They didn't know that I was still in the water and I couldn't swim out. About ten years after that, I thought, How did I come out of the water? Right to this day, I don't remember driving home or coming out of the lake. But I was out there having fun.

I had thirty-six old cars, and I lined them out. They would wreck my cars. I would take some to the shop. They sold some of my cars, and they sold my motor out of my cars. But I didn't feel bad about it because I used to take from people to. I was getting back what I did to people. But the cars didn't own me; I owned them.

Like I said, some people turned against me. They started calling me crazy, and passed by me in their cars. The devil turned a lot of my family against me. I started hearing voices and seeing things. I started hearing things in my house that I called the police. The police came to my house. They said, "That cane right there is your weapon." So I started carrying that cane everywhere I went.

That police was the devil, and I started jumping in front of people's cars and knocking people's truck and car windows out. Everybody would run when they see me. I could not take no more; police tried to stop me. I was fighting the police, and the next thing I know, they were taking me to a mental hospital. You see, the devil knew that I was going to find God, so he started messing with my mind. Now, I got my life together. I go around telling people who the devil is. They call me crazy. That has been the devil's plan—to make people think that I'm crazy because the devil doesn't want people to know he is Jesus. But I know who he is. He is the devil. I thought I was going down, but God was picking me up.

People always talk about the bad things you do, but they never talk about the good things you do. But everything is going to be alright after. Why? Because God promised that one day is not going to last forever. So have faith in God. Like I said, people started turning against me. But God will never turn against us. Whether we are good or bad, God is with us all the time. If God isn't a forgiving God, we all will be in trouble.

Sometimes, your family and your so-called friends can be your biggest downfall. I'm trying to get right with God. The devil ain't going to send them around me because I'm going to talk about God to them. As long as I was running around, they came. But like I said, my life started to change when I asked God to forgive me for my sin. I named all the sin that I did, and one morning, I got up, and God took all the drugs, cigarettes, drinking, and running around from me.

It has been fifteen years. I don't do none of that no more. If God has changed me, he can change anybody. Even with all the sins we did, God brought us a long way and would still caring us. God is with us, even if we are good or bad. Never give up on God because

God can do everything except to fail. That was how I knew that God didn't drown the world or did all that killing the Bible says he did. God is love. And I want to thank you, God, for everything. But most of all, I want to thank you for you, God. I love you, God, and I know you love us more. This is written by a man called Possum aka Larry Gene Baxter.

ABOUT THE AUTHOR

Larry Gene Baxter Sr. is a strong believer of God. He has been married for thirty-one years, and he thanks God for his wife daily. He has six children and thirteen grandchildren. God has brought him and his family a mighty long way, and he's still carrying them. Larry loves all of God's creations, but none of God's creations can compare to the love he has for the Creator!

9 7 9 8 8 8 8 9 4 3 9 2 5 7